Five Ways to Get the Upper Hand *Every* Time

Third Edition

by

Joseph A. Caruso

Brookshire Press

Copies of this book are available at special quantity discounts for sales promotions, corporations, and teaching institutions.

For details, write or telephone CarusoKlemans International Development Institute, Brookshire Press, 3171 Palmetto Court, Trenton, Michigan 48183. (313) 692-0544.

A Brookshire Press Publication of CarusoKlemans International Development Intstitute, 3171 Palmetto Court, Trenton, MI 48183.

ISBN: 1-885671-06-7
Printed in the U.S.A.

To Mickey Caruso

My friend
My teacher
My father

--

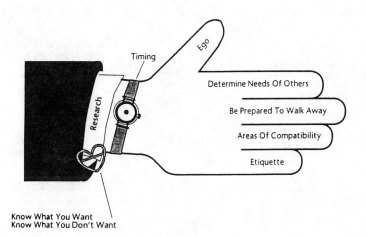

Timing

Ego

Determine Needs Of Others

Be Prepared To Walk Away

Areas Of Compatibility

Etiquette

Research

Know What You Want
Know What You Don't Want

"I have read '5 Ways to Get the Upper Hand Every Time.' I would recommend this book to not only negotiators and people in leadership roles, but also to anyone that wants to expand their interpersonal relationships."

Neil E. Van Riper
Superintendent of Schools

"'5 Ways to Get the Upper Hand Every Time' typifies what Joe Caruso does best: Taking complex issues and grinding them down to their essential elements. His 'hand' method points out all the land mines that stand in the way of successful negotiations."

Joe Hoshaw, Editor
The News-Herald Newspapers

"...excellent analysis enabling all of us to achieve our dreams."

Marvin Sonne, D.D.S.

"...clear, concise, and an easy read. Employers and employees alike can benefit greatly from reading this book and applying the easy to remember techniques."

Gregory Roche, D.O., P.C.

"The only thing I've found to be more effective than this book in helping us with employee relations as well as customer service was Caruso's on-site seminar."

Gary Weaver, President
H & W Investments

"'5 Ways to Get the Upper Hand Every Time' ranks among the most effective, easy to read, complete, and concise books on the subject."

Pat Klavitter
Program Coordinator
National Seminars

"A rational and thought provoking compendium of safe passageways through the negotiating mine field."

R.R. Manthey
Senior Consultant
Rollins, Burdick, Hunter Co.

"I wish I would have read this 20 years ago when I first started teaching -- A must read!"

Rick Goward
Director of Bands
Henry Ford Community College

"The book is a very good tool and practical. It's refreshing. So many books of this type are overly analytical."

Lorenzo Howard
Manager, Human Resources
BASF Corporation

"Life is a constant negotiation process. '5 Ways to Get the Upper Hand Every Time' reminds us of those things which are not always taught during a formal education but have a major impact on our lives. This book is a refreshing common sense approach that if used will improve our ability to successfully deal with ourselves and others."

Larry Fitch
City Administrator

"Joe Caruso provides more than a technique for successful negotiations. He shares his philosophy for negotiating through life with a healthy perspective and a good sense of humor."

Marsha Stopa, Editor
The News-Herald Newspapers

ACKNOWLEDGMENTS

This book would possibly have never been written without the strong conviction that each of us has a personal responsibility to positively grow and encourage positive growth; to love and to encourage love; to enjoy and encourage enjoyment.

I am fortunate to have a life in which I have been surrounded by caring people who serve as an inspiration for personal growth. The acknowledgments must begin with those who have actively participated in the creation of this book: Maria Ventura, my "right hand," without whom this book may still not be finished; Dave LaBeau for giving me the opportunity for development and exposure; Skip Cypert for providing the inspiration and support; Barbara Ludt for her generous and unending help; and John Walker, Lloyd Grace and the crew at Paragrafix, without whom this book could not have been printed.

I'd also like to take this opportunity to thank my friends and family: my brothers, my partners, and my friends -- Mike (thanks for the title), Dave and Rob; Sherry and Kim Caruso, the best sister-in-laws in the world; Barbara Klemans, my partner, teammate and friend; and Joe Hoshaw, the editor of my column, *Success Strategies*, and a very good friend. These acknowledgments would be longer than the contents of the book if I were to mention all of the wonderful people who have been a positive influence on me throughout my life. Without them, there may have never been a book at all. To all of these people, I will continue to give my respect, admiration, support and gratitude.

CONTENTS

FOREWORD

Many years ago, I had the dubious opportunity to work with an event promoter who learned the business traveling from town to town promoting county fairs. A complete wild man, personally, his years of experience had so honed his instincts about people and business deals that he could unmask a con artist in seconds and judge the merits of a proposal without ever reading it. He seldom miscalculated.

The old promoter had one simple rule from which he never deviated. He fervently believed and often said, "A deal is not a good deal unless it's a good deal for everyone involved." If one of the principals in a deal wanted to profit unfairly, he figured this was not the kind of guy he wanted to do business with. Likewise, if the deal was not structured so that it provided equal incentive for all parties involved, the arrangement -- whatever it was -- would not work as it should.

Like most profound truths, his was a simple idea. Yet, in a career that has for more than three decades allowed me to meet and work with business people, laborers, military personnel, students, government officials, and entertainers -- people from virtually every walk of life -- I continue to be amazed at how frequently people overlook or attempt to alter this simple truth. Following this single rule can make the difference between mediocrity, or even failure, and spectacular success.

In this book, Joe Caruso explores the strategies, tactics, and techniques that can help you to learn in an afternoon the skills that my old friend spent a lifetime perfecting. Negotiation, after all, is the art of making sure that you receive a fair shake in your work, your relationships, and in your life, and that you don't unfairly take advantage of others.

The techniques he discusses are supported with lively examples and illustrated with interesting case studies. Inspirational quotes help you remember key ideas and motivate yourself to ever higher levels of achievement. You can learn very quickly how to conduct yourself in a winning way, all the while keeping your eye on your goal, in order to ensure that you achieve the desired outcome in negotiations.

To aid in learning and recall, the book is built around a symbol of negotiation -- your hand. After you've completed this book, simply glancing at your hand will remind you of the concepts contained in Caruso's discussion of the fundamentals of negotiation. Best of all, the book will make you feel better about yourself. You will be stronger, more self-assured, and more persuasive -- confident that you have the courage of your convictions and certain knowledge that in the end you will strike a fair bargain.

You can put the ideas in this book to work immediately

to help achieve success in whatever you attempt.

Samuel Cypert, author
Believe and Achieve

Joseph A. Caruso

INTRODUCTION

I'd like to begin by congratulating you on taking a major step toward improving your quality of life through better everyday negotiations.

Let me qualify this by stating that I am not a genius and the information in this book has not been purely and immaculately conceived in original thought. I simply studied and analyzed what I found to be the most important and easily implemented philosophies and techniques for achieving successful negotiation skills. Then, I organized these thoughts into a manner that you will find easy to remember, retain and, most importantly, apply.

As you've probably noticed, the first several pages in this book contain many complimentary statements about its contents. The reason I decided to start the book with these comments is the same reason I decided to include so many of them...It's important that you *really believe* this information will help you in your personal and professional life.

I took the liberty of sending advanced copies to some people who are comfortable with the level of success and happiness they have achieved in their lives. I simply asked them to read the material and, if they were so inclined, to write me with their thoughts afterward. I decided to include these in the beginning of the book to build up your expectations. I want you to believe that the information will help you with your life. If you don't believe this book can help you, it won't. Simply reading it will not change your life in any way. In fact, this book can't change your life at all. **<u>You</u> must change your life.**

I've complemented you on taking the first step toward improving your quality of life by *reading* this book. That step, however, is absolutely worthless without the second and third steps: *retaining* the information and *applying it* when you need to.

You are obviously interested in improving your negotiation skills or you wouldn't be reading this right now. The techniques and ideas included here are applied daily by some of the most successful people in the world. They can, and will, help you. In order to gain the most benefit from this book, however, you must approach it with an open mind and the willingness to change.

Nineteenth century English economist Walter Bagehot once said, "One of the greatest pains to human nature is the pain of a new idea." I encourage you to approach this book with a *positive attitude* because it will greatly influence the effectiveness of the information. I urge you to read this book *actively*.

Five Ways to Get the Upper Hand Every Time

Read the ideas, thoughts, techniques and philosophies with the intent of applying them in your life. The Greek philosopher Plotinus said, "Knowledge without action is dead to us." I am confident that you will see a positive difference in your life by remembering and applying the techniques in this book.

I recently had an opportunity to present a seminar on negotiation to more than 50 CEOs from around the country. Collectively, these ladies and gentlemen had attended more than 1,500 seminars in their professional careers. I asked them two questions regarding the information in those seminars. First, "What percentage of the information do you remember?" The group arrived at a consensus of seven percent. The second question was, "What percentage of that seven percent are you able to apply in your daily lives?" The answer was astoundingly only one percent or lower.

Each year, millions and millions of dollars are spent by corporations, associations and clubs on seminars. Millions more are spent on self-help books. If you were able to remember and apply only one percent of the information contained in this book, I would consider it a miserable failure. Even the best information in the world is useless unless it is applied. For this reason, I decided the ideas in this book must be accompanied by a mechanism that will help you associate and assimilate them. I have chosen the hand as this mechanism.

Joseph A. Caruso

As you read each section, refer to your hand to help reinforce the ideas. After reading the book, refer to your hand when you need the information the most (like in the midst of a heated debate). By doing so, you will be able to quickly review the elements, ideas and techniques that will help you the most at that time.

The book is divided into four basic sections:

1. Before Hand
   - A. Know What You Want and Don't Want (Heart Cuff Link)
   - B. Research (Cuff of Sleeve)
   - C. Timing (Watch)

2. The Matter at Hand
   - A. Control Your Ego (Thumb)
   - B. Determine Needs Of Others (Index Finger)
   - C. Be Prepared To Walk Away (Middle Finger)
   - D. Look For Areas Of Compatibility (Ring Finger)
   - E. Use Etiquette (Little Finger)

3. Holding Your Hand
   - A. The Power of Habit: Knowing the power of habit will make you more successful in

5

incorporating the ideas and techniques of this book into your daily behavior.

B.   Decision vs. Commitment

4. A Helping Hand

A.   A collection of motivating and/or thought-provoking quotes. I have included these at the end of the book in hopes that one or more of them will stimulate action on your part. They may also help you keep your commitment to personal growth. At the very least, I hope you find them enjoyable.

For the most part, I try to avoid the cute pop terms and trendy labels employed by most self-help seminars and books. I know they help to sell books and are great fodder for talk shows; but I don't believe they do much to help us produce positive change in our lives.

Throughout the history of human existence, we've found ways to communicate with each other regardless of language, cultural, social, sexual or economic boundaries. Throughout time, the elements of successful interpersonal communication have not changed. These elements have remained the same because, in regard to interpersonal com-

Joseph A. Caruso

munication, the basic needs, fears and anxieties of individual human beings haven't changed. This book identifies and explains the most essential elements, areas and perspectives necessary for successful interpersonal communication or win-win negotiation.

As you read this book, pick up a pen and make specific notes to yourself. Take the time to expand on the information and compare it to your own experiences and/or thoughts.

Again, I congratulate you. By wanting to improve your life, and by actually taking steps to positively grow and expand your talents and abilities, you are setting yourself apart from most people. You are displaying some of the characteristics of the most successful people in the world. Let's begin...

WIN-WIN NEGOTIATION

This book is about negotiation. More specifically, it's about win-win negotiation. The information will allow you to achieve a higher level of success in your interpersonal relationships because negotiation skills have a positive and dramatic impact on your life. You will be happier, more in control and more successful in everything you do.

If this statement sounds overly optimistic, consider the following questions: What if every time you communicated with someone, you were more effective in getting what you wanted and you were able to help that person get what he or she wanted? What if, more often than not, you knew exactly what you wanted as well as exactly what you didn't want before negotiating? What if people were unable to push your buttons to elicit an emotional response during high-pressure negotiations?

It's a fact that successful negotiators feel more in control of their lives and less like victims. Successful win-win negotiators are generally well-liked and respected by others.

It's not a question of whether or not you negotiate, it's

how good you are when you do. There is an inherent danger of being in the midst of a negotiation and not recognizing it as such. Virtually all of your communication with other people is a form of negotiation.

You are the only one who can know exactly what you want and what you need. You are the only one who has the bottom-line responsibility of making sure you get it. This book is not about taking advantage of people to get what you want in life. It's about *win-win* negotiation.

There are five basic characteristics of a successful, win-win negotiation:

1. Both sides feel a sense of accomplishment.
2. Both sides feel the other side cared.
3. Both sides feel the other side was fair.
4. Each side would deal again with the other.
5. Each side feels the other side will keep the bargain.

A win-win negotiation has as much to do with helping your counterparts get what they want as it does with helping you get what you want. It is not beneficial, nor is it necessary, for negotiation to be stressful, oppositional and/or confrontational. I realize you will not be in the fortunate position of having everyone you negotiate with understand and practice

Five Ways to Get the Upper Hand Every Time

win-win negotiation skills. More often than not, you will find that your counterparts don't realize that it's in their best interest to determine your goals in the negotiation, let alone to help provide the circumstances that will allow you to achieve them. For this reason, it is even more important that you develop the skills that will allow you to get what you want *and* let your counterparts get what they want.

According to Roger Dawson, author of *The Secrets of Power in Negotiating*, there are five things that make a good negotiator:

1.   Knowing that both sides are under pressure so you don't feel intimidated
2.   Wanting to learn negotiating skills
3.   Understanding negotiating skills
4.   Being willing to practice
5.   Wanting to create win-win negotiating situations

Quite often I am invited to speak to various businesses and associations about different interpersonal communication skills. On all of these occasions, I feel I have two main responsibilities. The first is to provide pertinent information in an entertaining manner. The second is to provide my audience with a mechanism that will allow them to retain and retrieve the information easily.

Like my seminars, the information in this book will be presented in such a way that -- if you choose to -- you will not only remember the basic principles of win-win negotiation, but you will have a mechanism in place to apply them when you need them the most.

Section I

PREPARATION
(Before Hand)

Joseph A. Caruso

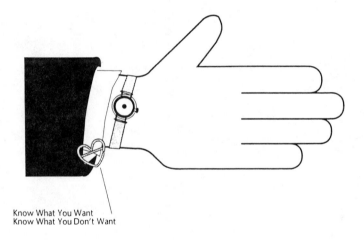

Know What You Want
Know What You Don't Want

Chapter 1

KNOW WHAT YOU WANT
AND DON'T WANT

Before you enter into any negotiation, you need to consider three factors that will greatly affect your ability to negotiate successfully.

First, you have to *know what you want and what you won't accept.* This is symbolized by the heart-shaped cuff link on the illustration.

Much has been written about the importance of well-defined goals. You must know specifically what you want to achieve from the negotiation. Be realistic. Going into a negotiation saying, *"I know what I want...I want whatever I get,"* is not laying the groundwork for successful negotiation. As you determine what you want, think positively. Don't make decisions for your counterparts ("I know they probably won't say yes to this..." or "I highly doubt I'll be able to get this...").

14

Joseph A. Caruso

Respect your counterparts enough to allow them to make their own decisions. Determine clear, concise and realistic goals and **WRITE THEM DOWN**.

Please understand that just because you should define what you want, this does not, under any circumstances, imply that the first step of negotiation is to *tell* your counterparts what you want. **NEVER BE THE FIRST TO STATE WHAT YOU WANT.**

EXAMPLE: A gentleman named Brian Epstein managed a "marginally successful rock group" called The Beatles. At the time of this story, The Beatles had already achieved a tremendously higher amount of success than any other band in the history of popular music. The executives at the American film studio (which shall remain nameless) were very interested in getting The Beatles to sign with them for their first movie. On this day, prior to the negotiation, all of the executives in the studio were gathered in the board room, waiting for Mr. Epstein's arrival. The head of the studio turned to all of his employees and stated, "Gentlemen, this English manager chap has taken this band to heights never heard of in popular music, so he must be an extremely sharp and crafty negotiator. No matter what tactics he uses, and no matter how good he is, I'm not going to go over one million dollars in our offer to The Beatles." Everyone around the room agreed and made a mental note to be his best during this negotiation. A short time later, Brian Epstein walked into the board room. Introductions were made, and finally, the negotiation process began. The vice president of the motion picture company stood up to make his well-rehearsed opening statement..."Mr. Epstein, on behalf of our company, we would like to..." With a resounding thud, Epstein slammed his fist onto the tabletop and abruptly interrupted, "Gentlemen, before we begin, I think it only fair that I inform you that The Beatles are indisputably the most popular band in the world and we will not settle for a penny less than one hundred thousand dollars." His counterparts looked at each other incredulously. Did they hear him right? (They were prepared to pay over ten times that amount.)

LESSON: Brian Epstein knew exactly what he wanted before he went into the negotiation. However, he made the fatal mistake of sharing it with his counterparts *before* he found out what they were prepared to offer.

Once you have a clear picture of what you want, you must also know what you *don't* want, or your *Lowest Acceptable Situation* **(LAS).** How many times have you seen someone attempt to improve an existing situation only to eventually end up with either the same problems, similar problems or a situation that's worse than the first one? This generally happens when you fail to identify what you don't want -- or what is unacceptable -- prior to the negotiation. Sometimes we are so unhappy with our current situation that we are willing to accept almost anything that even vaguely promises a change in our circumstances.

EXAMPLE: An employee goes into his boss's office to ask for a raise because he doesn't feel he is advancing as quickly as he should within the organization. Rather than providing him with a raise, the boss offers a new title and the opportunity to work on a new project that, if successful, will be a tremendous "feather in his cap" and a catalyst for "great career advancement." The employee, dazzled by being offered such an important project and blinded by getting a new title, gladly accepts.

LESSON: Because the employee did not define ahead of time what he didn't want (or his LAS), the employer, being a good negotiator, was able to dazzle and distract him without ever really addressing his needs. What the employee actually did was continue to perpetuate all of his existing problems without getting his needs met. The bottom line: He accepted additional work, but he didn't receive an increase in compensation. He accepted a situation that held promise, but did not address his original concerns.

<u>REVIEW</u>

The first of three crucial elements in preparing for successful negotiation is:

Know what you want and don't want.

1.   WRITE IT DOWN!

2.   Define your LAS (Lowest Acceptable Situation)

Joseph A. Caruso

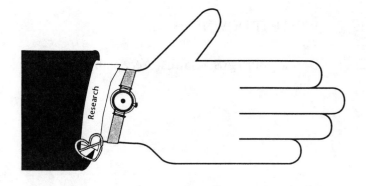

Chapter 2

RESEARCH

The second factor you must consider to successfully prepare for a win-win negotiation is *research*. This is represented by the cuff on the diagram.

Learn what you can about your counterparts: their likes, dislikes, negotiation style, background, histories, hobbies, etc. Understand that, as you're learning these things about your counterparts, all the information is coming to you second-hand and shouldn't necessarily be accepted as established fact. All of the information that you will be receiving will probably be heavily flavored with the personal interpretation of the person you're getting it from. So, whenever possible, try to get more than one source and consider the personalities of the sources. In addition, consider the relationship of each source with the people you're researching. Just like anything else in life, don't take this information out of context. At best, it will provide you with a general understanding of your counterparts.

Joseph A. Caruso

Another area that must be researched is the subject matter. Make sure you determine all of the variables involved. The more knowledgeable you are about your subject matter prior to a negotiation, the more respect you will command from your counterparts. (This will prevent you from making "off the **cuff**" remarks -- remember the diagram.)

One of the greatest sources of power you can have in a negotiation is a *Best Alternative to the Negotiated Agreement* (**BANA**). In other words, what if you did walk away? What is your best alternative if, in fact, a negotiated agreement can't be reached? According to Roger Fisher, William Ury and Bruce Patton, authors of the book *Getting to Yes*, a BANA is perhaps the most effective tool you can have when dealing with a seemingly more powerful negotiator. The more easily and happily you can walk away from a negotiation, the greater capacity you will have to affect its outcome.

EXAMPLE: Mike walked into his boss's office to ask for a raise. His boss asked, "Why should I give you a raise?" Mike replied, "Because I can work just about anywhere else, doing the same work I do here, or maybe even less work, and still get paid more money." His boss answered, "Fine. Go do it."

LESSON: Mike had absolutely no idea what the market would bear. His boss probably knew that the average salaries for comparable positions in competitive businesses were *less* than he was paying Mike. Because Mike didn't do any research, he would probably have to acquiesce and relinquish all positions.

I would be doing you a disservice if I didn't stress that most people will not take the time to research their *best alternative to a negotiated agreement.* More often than not, their undue optimism puts them at a disadvantage later on in the negotiation. They may believe that they have a great number of options, but, in actuality, they're under the influence of their imagined cumulative total, or the aggregate. I suggest you generate a list of your best alternatives, considering:

1.   Actions that you might take if you can't reach a negotiated agreement
2.   Play acting on some of these ideas to determine where they might lead
3.   What new opportunities they may bring to your life
4.   Tentatively selecting the option that seems to be the best

What I'm suggesting, in short, is to make your best alternatives*viabilities*, rather than*possibilities.* This will give you greater confidence and more power in your negotiation, which will be easily perceived by the other party through your verbal and nonverbal communications.

Once you feel you have totally researched your BANA, consider what your counterparts' BANA might be and do the same kind of research with theirs.

<u>REVIEW</u>

The second crucial element in preparing for a successful negotiation is:

Research!

1. Your counterparts

2. Your subject matter

3. Your *best alternative to a negotiated agreement* (BANA)

4. Your counterparts' BANA

Joseph A. Caruso

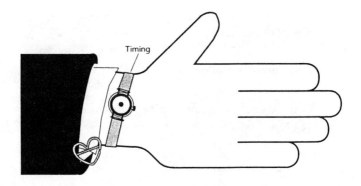

Timing

Chapter 3

TIMING

The third factor you must consider to successfully prepare for win-win negotiation is *timing*. This is represented by the watch on the diagram. (Surprise!)

The following should be answered in regard to timing: First, is it a good time to negotiate? Consider the general climate and its potential impact on your subject matter. Does it favor your position?

Secondly, how does the timing affect you? Are you rushed? Can you wait? Do you need a settlement immediately in order to solve your particular problems?

Thirdly, how does it affect your counterparts? Are they rushed? Do they need immediate results? Can they wait?

EXAMPLE: In the late 1960s, President Lyndon Johnson was determined to reach a negotiated settlement to the Vietnam War before the end of his presidency. He called his

Joseph A. Caruso

Secretary of State, Dean Rusk, and told him to take action in this regard. (This was the impetus for the Paris Peace Talks.) Rusk and the United States delegation went to France and rented an entire floor in one of the finest hotels in Paris -- on a *week-by-week* basis. The Vietnamese, on the other hand, went out to the French country-side and *purchased* a villa. The Vietnamese then began the negotiation by arguing about the shape of the table the negotiators would sit around.

LESSON: The Vietnamese delegation realized that Johnson was under tremendous time constraints and that they could use this as a form of power and leverage. And, as we know, Johnson was unsuccessful in negotiating an end to the Vietnam War.

Just as you'd *never* be the first to tell your counterparts what you want (unless you're feigning a limited-time offer in order to induce them into immediate action), *never* let your counterparts know your actual time constraints.

<u>REVIEW</u>

Important aspects in regard to timing are:

Timing:

1.   Review the climate.

2.   Review the deadlines, in terms of each party and how they may affect each position.

3.   Never communicate your deadline to your counterparts.

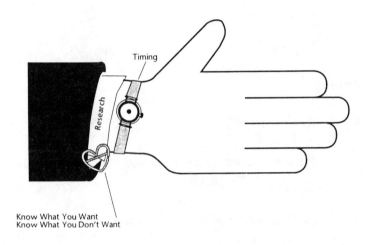

Timing

Research

Know What You Want
Know What You Don't Want

BEFORE HAND

These three areas of preparation can be crucial to effecting a successful win-win negotiation and should be given a great amount of consideration *"before hand."*

<u>REVIEW</u>

Three areas of preparation:

1.   Know what you want and don't want

2.   Research

3.   Timing

Joseph A. Caruso

Section II

NEGOTIATION
(The Matter At Hand)

Joseph A. Caruso

CONTROL YOUR EGO

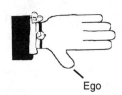

Ego

33

Chapter 4

CONTROL YOUR EGO
(Thumb)

The first factor in developing successful negotiation skills involves your *ego*. This is represented by the thumb.

Most mistakes in day-to-day negotiations can be traced to the fact that the "losers" let their egos get involved. When I refer to the word "ego," I'm not referring to one's "self-esteem" or "sense of self." It is important that one's self-love and self-esteem are intact and formidable. As Will Durant stated in his book, *The Story Of Philosophy,* "In some, egotism is a compensation for the absence of fame; in others, egotism lends generous cooperation to its presence." A "healthy ego" can actually be an asset to one's character. The Greek philosopher Cicero said, "Even the philosophers who write books in praise of humility take care to put their names on the title page."

Joseph A. Caruso

It is the unhealthy ego that is our worst enemy in a negotiation. It is the fragile, bloated, distorted, weak sense of self-importance that we need to address. I'm referring to one's *lack* of self-esteem. I'm referring to the part of us that feels we must tell someone who we are or what we stand for, because we obviously aren't communicating it well enough by just ***being*** who we are and ***doing*** what we stand for. Emerson said, "What you do speaks so loudly that I cannot hear what you say." This chapter deals with the part of our character that forces us to react quickly and, more often than not, predictably to provocation because of our ego.

Rule one: *Your attitudes will definitely affect your objectives.*

William James, the father of American psychology, stated that the most important discovery of our time is that ***we can only alter our lives by altering our attitudes.*** Popular motivational speaker Zig Ziglar says, "Your attitude is more important than your aptitude."

How many times have you been in a negotiation, whether it be with your wife, your husband, your boyfriend, your girlfriend, someone at work or your children, and your counterpart was able to "push your button," or say something

35

Five Ways to Get the Upper Hand Every Time

that set you off? So what happened? Well, more than likely you didn't handle the situation as well as you could have. This is called reacting rather than responding. (We've all been there.)

Unfortunately, in a negotiation, this will be your worst enemy. Your ego will make it virtually impossible for you to keep your mind on the issue and pay attention to your counterparts' needs. Your desire to achieve a win-win outcome will be greatly weakened when your "delicate ego" takes a "perceived hit" from your counterparts. You'll find yourself easily distracted from your objective every time.

Think back on the times in your recent past when this has happened to you. I'll venture a guess that, in the majority of those negotiations, not only didn't you enjoy the process, you didn't feel good about it afterward and, most importantly, you didn't achieve your objective. Essentially, you gave your counterparts your emotional "gearshift" and allowed them to put you in any emotional state they chose. Once they had you there, they made it virtually impossible for you to think clearly and use all of your abilities to achieve your goal.

Rule two: *Don't give anyone your emotional gearshift.*

Not letting other people control your emotions in a

negotiation may sound like an impossible task, but I assure you it isn't. Although it will require diligent practice, it is centered around a very simple and basic principle. You will find countless opportunities to apply it. The trick is looking for them, recognizing them, and acting on them. "The world isn't a playground, it's a schoolroom. And life is not a holiday, but an education."

Think about what makes a good athlete -- *practice*. What makes a good artist, a good sculptor, a good musician, a good linguist, a good stenographer? Practice, nothing else. If you don't exercise your arm, you don't get good biceps. If you take every opportunity, or even every other opportunity, to exercise one simple principle, you will find that you will achieve more success in getting what you want and more success in making other people happy. The by-products of both of those will bring more happiness into your life.

What's the simple technique? *"Respond rather than react."*

In 604 B.C., Lao Tzu, a Chinese philosopher, was credited with saying, "Respond rather than react." A response is an action, based on thought and premeditation, whereas a reaction is based largely on emotion.

Think back, again, to all of those times that you reacted negatively. Think about how much more successful you would

Five Ways to Get the Upper Hand Every Time

have been in the negotiation and how much more powerful you would have been if you would have responded rather than reacted.

You'll find that choosing a response is very easy and very common when you're negotiating with someone who is being pleasant. The challenge lies in being able to respond, rather than react, when you're dealing with someone who is being something less than pleasant. I'll guess that this was the case with most of the negotiations that I asked you to reflect on earlier. These people offer us the greatest opportunity for growth in regard to controlling our ego. I fondly refer to these situations as *"The Butthead Factor."*

The Butthead Factor refers to the fact that almost everyone will contest that they would be much happier, more productive and more successful if it weren't for those all-too-frequent occasions when they're forced to deal (negotiate) with less-than-pleasant people. What if you could apply a mechanism that would allow you to learn (with practice) how to respond, rather than react, in those situations? This is not an impossibility. It doesn't require extensive research in psychological behavior patterns or even years studying inter-personal communication techniques. As a matter of fact, the key was presented way back in 604 B.C. by our old friend Lao Tzu, who recommended that we:

Joseph A. Caruso

"Respond intelligently even to the unintelligent."

Think about it. There must have been buttheads back in 604 B.C. or old Lao Tzu never would have seen a need to offer this kind of advice. You see, the secret is that you can't change anyone but yourself. You can only hope to, at best, influence others by your behavior.

If you can take every opportunity during the day to remind yourself of this fact, and then choose to respond intelligently even to the unintelligent, the buttheads of the world will have a much more difficult time in eliciting a reaction, rather than a response, from you. This will allow you the opportunity to achieve a win-win negotiation much more consistently and be happier in the process.

If this sounds too simple, or unrealistic, think about the facts:
1.   Buttheads have been here for thousands of years.
2.   You can't change them.
3.   You can't remove them.
4.   You can only control yourself.

Rule three: *Respond intelligently even to the unintelligent.*

Five Ways to Get the Upper Hand Every Time

The most powerful and most effective technique to use when people start to get confrontational in a negotiation is to *respond* by staying with the issue. Refrain from taking offense and from wanting to *react* by attacking them. If your self-esteem is where it should be, it's in a place where they can't get to it. Think about that. It runs so strong and so deep that simple comments or emotionally driven remarks will not be any test.

How do you get to the point where you are almost impervious to petty personal attacks? You have to practice responding rather than reacting with every opportunity. With each successful application...a victory. Each small victory will build upon the next, until this behavior pattern manifests itself and becomes apparent in your character. Remember Goethe's words of wisdom, "Talent develops itself in solitude; character in the stream of life." There is no other way to build character than by taking these situations one at a time as they present themselves, approaching them as opportunities to build your self-esteem and develop a character that allows you to eventually respond intelligently even to the unintelligent with less and less effort.

I can tell you from personal experience that I take every opportunity to apply this philosophy. It is not always easy, but the rewards are always fantastic. My friends, relatives and closest confidants can attest to the fact that I have reacted rather than responded -- or given people my emotional gear-shift -- less than a handful of times in the past year (and I'll guarantee you that the butthead factor in my life during this time hasn't changed). This is coming from a person who embarrassingly admits that he once hurt his hand hitting a wall because someone said something that made him so mad he didn't know what else to do. That type of reaction is not conducive to achieving a win-win negotiation, let alone gaining respect.

Most of the time, you'll find yourself negotiating with people who apparently have not given a great deal of attention to their negotiation skills or their development in interpersonal communication. The negotiation process is not the time to teach them a lesson, nor is it the time to point out any perceived flaws or weaknesses you may think they have. *Stay focused on your goal of achieving a win-win negotiation.* For the last time, I will refer to some very wise words from our friend Lao Tzu that may help you in these situations. They have helped me tremendously.

If you see what is small as it sees itself / and accept what is weak for the strength it has / and use what is dim for the light it gives, / then all will go well. / This is called acting naturally.

Five Ways to Get the Upper Hand Every Time

Avoid focusing your thoughts on whether or not someone is treating you as well as you feel you deserve to be treated. Don't give your counterparts credit when they don't have the behavioral collateral. Simply accept the situation for what it is. Don't try to change them as people. Simply try to influence them with your most intelligent and carefully chosen response. Set an example for them. I think you will be pleasantly surprised to find that, if you don't allow yourself to be blinded by emotions, you will easily find the right answer and choose the right response that will allow you to move closer to achieving your goal.

When your counterparts lash out with remarks or strong words meant to make you flinch, recoil, or even hurt enough that you are distracted from your goal, you will find the strongest, most powerful and effective weapon doesn't come from a counterattack. Rather, it comes from letting those words and remarks become impotent because they can't find their target -- your ego. Confucius is credited with saying, "To be wronged is nothing unless you continue to remember it."

The more successful you are at controlling your ego, the more successful you'll be at identifying when others are not controlling theirs. In an overwhelming majority of the cases, when people let their egos get involved and allow their emotions to run their show, it's usually because they perceive the other party to be more powerful in some regard. Nothing induces emotional response more than a sense of frustration. Frustration is born from a perception that you lack the ability to control a situation.

EXAMPLE: Perhaps the best example of someone who achieved phenomenal results through peaceful negotiation by controlling the ego was Mahatma Gandhi when he was negotiating with the British Empire for the independence of India. Most of the world perceived Gandhi to be at a tremendous disadvantage. Gandhi was a very religious man with deep non-confrontational and nonviolent convictions. He was representing a country that had 17 states, 21 languages, hundreds of dialects, many religions and no means of mass communication to the majority of the people. His opponent, the British Empire, was, at the time, one of the most powerful countries in the world. It was more organized and, on the whole, more educated. Gandhi, at first, merely amused the British. Then he befuddled them, amazed them and, finally, overcame them by consistently and continually communicating to them that they, in fact, were the ones with the problem. He let them know that it was actually in their best interest to come up with a solution that would be in Gandhi's and India's best interests. In the end, India won its independence. Gandhi was, and still is, one of the most respected men who ever lived, even by his opponents.

Five Ways to Get the Upper Hand Every Time

LESSON: Power is perceived. Stay true to your objective of achieving a win-win negotiation and don't be distracted by cheap shots, attempts to make you react, or temptations to teach your counterparts a lesson.

      T.H. Huxley once said, "When you cannot prove that people are wrong, but only that they are absurd, the best course is to let them alone." When it comes to negotiation, this technique can be extremely effective and quite simple to apply. If, in fact, your counterparts state something ridiculous about a specific issue, or take an unrealistic stance, let it alone. Come back to it. Say something like, "Let's move on. We can always come back to that later." If you continue to be consistent with them and are successful in other areas of the negotiation as it progresses, you'll find their stand on that particular issue will soften tremendously and, in most cases, go away.

      If tempers get hot and you perceive that your counterparts' emotions may have a greater determination over their behavior than their logic, there is another simple technique you can apply. Simply repeat what they have stated back to them in the form of a question and allow them to hear how ridiculous it is.

      If you feel your energy level starting to rise, simply pause and count to three after each of their statements, before you begin to speak. When you do speak, talk a little more quietly and a little more slowly. This will slow the tempo of the conversation. It will also give you time to think and lower your emotional level before you open your mouth.

CAUTION: Be careful not to speak too slowly and too quietly. That might make it appear as if you're trying to teach them a lesson. Simply slow down a notch or two. Quiet down a decibel or so below theirs and continue to come down a little at a time. They will perceive the difference in your tone and tempo and more than likely they will start to change their own.

A third technique, and one I use often, works when you find that their emotional level is affecting their ability to negotiate. It's a simple statement: "I can appreciate that you're very involved with this and I know that it's got you upset, but we should really try to stick with the issue to see if we can get this resolved." Always stick with the issue. Try to take personalities out of the picture. Let them know you respect that the issue is important to them, that it is also important to you, and that you're both there to try to fix things, not perpetuate any adverse effects the existing conditions have had on each of you. Always go back to the issue.

If you reach a point where you can't provide them with

Five Ways to Get the Upper Hand Every Time

some emotional distance, you can't divert their attention, they won't allow you to change the subject, and none of the techniques above have worked, the best action may be to postpone the negotiation. Tell them you'll have to get back with them. Tell them you're out of time, but don't lead them to believe that the reason you're postponing has anything to do with them or their emotional state. Avoid comments like, "Well, we'll talk about this after you calm down."

Joseph A. Caruso

In infancy the thumb provided so many of us with great security as we suckled it. As adults, it continues to offer us great security by reminding us that one of the biggest impediments to successful interpersonal communication and win-win negotiation is our ego.

<u>REVIEW</u>

Ego (Thumb):

1.   *Respond* rather than *react.*

2.   *Attitude* is more important than *aptitude.*

3.   Respond *intelligently* even to the *unintelligent.*

4.   Don't let *emotion* control the negotiation.

5.   Stick to the *issue.*

Joseph A. Caruso

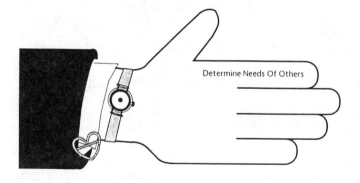

Determine Needs Of Others

Chapter 5

DETERMINE NEEDS
OF OTHERS
(Index Finger)

The second most important approach to successful negotiation is represented by your index finger.

This finger represents: *determining the needs of your counterparts.* Since I'm in the marketing business, I'd like to share an old marketing axiom with you: "Give people what they want, and you'll be successful. Give people what they need, and you'll be successful beyond your wildest dreams."

In order for you to give people what they want, or what they need, you must first be able to determine what they want, or what they need. Because it is sometimes much more difficult to determine people's needs, it is usually best to first determine what they want. The easiest and most effective way to determine the wants of other people comprises a very simple

Joseph A. Caruso

two-step process:
1. Ask them.
2. Listen.

EXAMPLE: This reminds me of a story about a brand new restaurant that was opening in town. Prior to the opening, the owner of the restaurant had a meeting with all of the employees and told them that his goal was to provide outstanding food and superior service. He said, "I don't care what it takes; I don't want any customers in this restaurant to be unhappy." Shortly after the meeting, it was time to open the doors and let the first customer in. The customer was greeted warmly by the host and shown to an elegant table. He ordered what he hoped would be a delicious meal. The waiter soon appeared with the soup the gentleman ordered and with a flair he placed it in front of the customer. He then left the customer alone to eat his soup. Within minutes he came back and noticed that the customer had not yet begun to eat the soup. With great concern he asked the customer, "Sir, is there something wrong?" The customer replied, "Absolutely. I just can't eat this soup." The waiter, remembering that the owner wanted to give the impression that the restaurant will do everything it can to provide the customer with superior service, thought quickly and decided to call over the head-waiter. (This is called passing the buck.) The head-waiter came up and said, "Can I help you, sir?" The customer replied, "As I told your waiter, I simply can't eat this soup." The head-waiter said, "Yes, sir. I'm sorry, sir. I'll be right back." Then he disappeared. Moments later, he returned with the chef. The chef looked at the customer and said, "Is there something wrong with the soup?" To that the customer answered, "Yes, sir, there is. As I told the waiters, it's impossible for me to eat this soup." The chef calmly asked a one-word question..."Why?" The customer replied, "I have no spoon."

Ask people what they want. If they don't communicate clearly what they want, or they seem to be jumping from issue to issue and aren't being specific enough, continue to ask them more focused questions until their desires become apparent.

The process of listening, then asking another question, then listening, then asking another question, until you get them to focus in on the issue, the problem and their desires, is called *active* listening. It's like a talk-show host interviewing a guest: Ask a question, actively listen to the response, then ask the next question based on any ambiguous or leading thoughts they may have given you. Then repeat the process. Pay attention to the direction they take the subject matter, the energy level of their response and the conviction of their tone.

A good technique is to begin with open questions and then move to closed questions. An open question begins with words like how, why, what, where, etc. An open question cannot be simply answered with a yes or no. Instead, it requires an answer that provides a more elaborate response. A closed question begins with do, can, will, should, have, etc. These questions allow your counterparts to answer with a yes or no and will greatly help you to determine their position on issues as well as their needs and wants.

As I indicated earlier, it is important to pay attention to their nonverbal, as well as their verbal, communication. We're all actors at heart. William James once said that when two people meet, there are actually six people meeting: each person the way they see themselves, each person as they really are, and each person the way the other person sees them.

Try not to assume that it's your counterparts' responsibility to tell you what they want or to make their needs evident. In fact, it isn't. It's *your* responsibility to be able to make those determinations. Sometimes your counterparts will become frustrated by their inability to effectively communicate their needs to you. This may cause them to either withdraw or verbally lash out. Bear in mind it is *not* in your best interest to help them communicate to you that they lack technique. It will behoove you to accept their limitations as communicators rather than make them the issue. Maslow said, "If the only tool you have is a hammer, you tend to treat everything as if it were

Five Ways to Get the Upper Hand Every Time

a nail." Challenge their limits and your techniques by searching for a way that you can help them with your "mutual problem." This is not the time to be judgmental.

Successful people take 100 percent responsibility for communication. Plato said, "A man who makes everything that leads to happiness depend upon himself and not upon other people, has adopted the best plan for living happily." Take full responsibility for determining their needs. Don't hold them responsible for the fact that they may not be able to clearly communicate what they need or what they want. You may need to pull it out of them. They may be hiding it from you for a specific reason or they may just be earnestly unaware. Pay attention. Listen actively. Have a sincere desire to determine their needs. Try to look at the issue from their viewpoint and with their perspective. Keep reminding yourself that your goal is to achieve a win-win negotiation. If, for whatever reason, you fall short in your efforts to determine the needs of your counterparts, the outcome will *not* be a win-win negotiation.

It's been my experience, over years of practice, that when I have a sincere desire to determine, understand and appreciate the needs of others, I am extremely effective in not only helping them achieve their goals, but also in persuading them to help me achieve mine. Even with the most difficult counterparts, I remind myself that my challenge for personal growth is to successfully determine their needs so that I can help them get what they want. Zig Ziglar says, "You can have anything you want in life, if you help enough people get what they want."

If, in fact, your counterparts are so worked up that, when you ask them what they want, they end up making demands or ridiculous statements, ask them to suggest possible solutions. If they're very bitter, their communication skills are poor, their negotiation skills are poor, their ego is in the way, they're upset, they're hardlining you or they're using cheap tactics, try not to make judgments. Instead, focus in on your genuine care for their needs and realize that the more successful you are at determining and providing for their needs, the more opportunity you'll have for being successful in the negotiation.

AREA FOR CONCERN: There may be times when you find yourself coming off in a condescending manner. In these instances, *actively involve* your counterparts in the process of helping *them* solve *their* problem. Realize that their needs are just as important to them as yours are to you. If you find yourself in a position where you don't care as much as you think you should, go back to our discussion on the ego (thumb) and address *your* problems. Think about our friend Lao Tzu. Think about responding intelligently. Remind yourself again that the

Five Ways to Get the Upper Hand Every Time

best possible outcome in this negotiation is not only for you to get what you want, but for them to get what they want. Know that, if you can help them determine their needs, this will help you in your life.

There may be times when you find that your counter-parts' needs or wants are intangible.

EXAMPLE: In this instance, Mr. Smith should not acknowledge that he knows what Mr. Green needs. Rather, he should make Mr. Green "feel" that he is right; that he is teaching Mr. Smith a lesson, and that Mr. Smith is grateful for the opportunity to have learned something in the process. By doing this, Mr. Green's needs (determined by his ego and insecurity) have been addressed and satiated. He will be much more willing to acquiesce to Mr. Smith's desires.

Never belittle your counterparts. Everyone likes to be right. Everyone likes to be validated. People like to feel that they're the ones being benevolent or that they're on the winning side. You very rarely have anything to gain by belittling your counterparts or making them feel inferior.

If you truly and successfully addressed the No. 1 philosophy behind negotiation (your ego/thumb), you will have a much greater opportunity for success with the No. 2 philosophy (determining people's needs/index finger).

Joseph A. Caruso

CAUTION: It is virtually impossible to determine the needs of our counterparts -- let alone provide them with situations they will find acceptable -- unless our own egos remain in check.

Five Ways to Get the Upper Hand Every Time

<u>REVIEW</u>

Determine Needs Of Others:

1. To determine your counterparts' needs, ask them.

2. Listen actively.

3. Use open and closed questions.

4. Take 100 percent responsibility for your communication.

5. Never belittle your counterparts.

Joseph A. Caruso

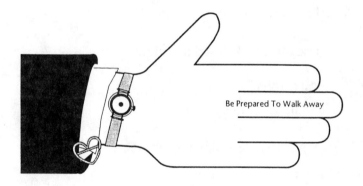

Be Prepared To Walk Away

Chapter 6

BE PREPARED
TO WALK AWAY
(Middle Finger)

The third most important element in our quest for a win-win negotiation is represented by the middle finger: *be prepared to walk away.*

The effort you put into researching your *best alternative to a negotiated agreement* (BANA) prior to a negotiation will determine the effectiveness of this technique. As I said in the chapter titled "Research," the more easily and happily you can walk away from a negotiation, the greater your capacity to affect the outcome.

You need to research your BANA thoroughly to be able to successfully communicate to your counterparts that you are, in fact, prepared to walk away. With proper preparation, your willingness to walk away will be communicated without

60

Joseph A. Caruso

you ever having to *say* that you are willing to walk away. Researching your BANA will allow you to approach the negotiation with confidence and security. Please don't misinterpret this. I am not recommending that you try to intimidate your counterparts with this technique. However, it is crucial that your counterparts value your participation and know that your participation is a commodity that should not be taken for granted.

It is human nature for us to try to take advantage of people we know we can. By this, I'm not implying we are all greedy, uncaring, selfish individuals. Perhaps my point is best communicated by the following behavioral analysis.

EXAMPLE: Think of all your interpersonal relationships, starting with the least familiar (people you've just met) to your most familiar (people you live with). Isn't it true that, in most cases, we have a tendency to show those whom we've just met our best side, while we take less care to shield those who are closest to us from our "little character imperfections?" (Remember the song, "You Always Hurt the One You Love?") I believe this is because we have an innate ability to subconsciously evaluate the other person's level of commitment to our relationship. We then match that level of commitment with an inverse amount of "behavioral restraint." In other words, we know the amount of frequency or intensity that we will be allowed to "misbehave" with that person, based on his/her tolerance with us. In a large number of cases, that person's tolerance must factor in the level of commitment he/she has in the relationship. People we've just met have very little commitment to our relationship, so we usually give them our best.

This philosophy can easily be applied to the process of negotiation. If you have done a good job researching your BANA, you will communicate this fact in many ways (i.e., your posture, approach, excitement level, patience, common sense and ability to keep an emotional distance from the subject matter). These communications show them that you are prepared to walk away from the negotiation at any moment. You are not communicating this with malice, nor in any overt sense. This will influence your counterparts' behavior in such a way that they will work hard to treat you with respect (as they would the stranger whose level of commitment in the relationship is less than a family member's).

The simple fact is, people can't take advantage of you unless you give them permission and you somehow communicate to them that they can.

This technique is very successful in family and close personal relationships as well. Your friends and relatives will treat you with more respect and show more care and affection the more they value your involvement in the relationship. I might add that you should work just as hard at letting them know how much you value their involvement in the relationship. (Let's face it, no one likes to be taken for granted.) In a negotiation, you would be doing your counterparts a disservice if you took them for granted. Unfortunately, you can't count on the fact that your counterparts will have read and applied the techniques in this book. Therefore, you must do everything in your power to communicate to them that it's in their best interest not to take you for granted.

The walk-away technique can be used in many ways and can range from "I'll get back to you" to "I'm afraid we've reached an impasse at this time. Thank you very much for your consideration." However, it's important to not overuse this technique. You must carefully monitor your timing and frequency. A good way to make sure you're not overusing this technique is to ask yourself whether you're using it just to "posture" or manipulate your counterparts. Rather, you should use this technique because you believe it's in your counterparts' best interest that you leave the negotiation for a short period of time or because you've determined that your counterparts are not, at least for now, interested in negotiating with you in good faith.

Consider also that good negotiators rarely make deci-

Five Ways to Get the Upper Hand Every Time

sions on the spot. The psychological pressure to be nice and give in when you're in front of your counterparts is far too great. Time and distance help separate personalities and pressure tactics from the problem and the best solution.

Good negotiators come to the table with credible reasons in their pockets for leaving whenever they want. An excellent excuse to leave the negotiation for a short period of time is to defer the ultimate decision to a third party. This will help disarm your counterparts from trying to force you into a decision or win you over based on emotional reactions. Allude to the fact that you must check with someone else for an ultimate decision. This forces your counterparts to be more clear, more concise, more emphatic and less emotional with their specific points. They need to increase their chances that you will communicate *their* side and *their* perspective to your ultimate decision maker.

CAUTION: Your reasons for deferring the decision to a third party should not be indicative of an inability to make a decision. It's still important that you show decisiveness and control throughout the negotiation. Use this technique as an opportunity to show how much you respect your counterparts and that you will communicate their perspective in a fair, just and unbiased manner.

Joseph A. Caruso

REVIEW

Be Prepared To Walk Away:

1. Your ability to walk away is based on the amount of time and effort you put into your BANA at the research stage.

2. Don't overuse this technique.

3. Be very careful with your timing.

4. Don't flaunt it. Be careful to communicate respect while indicating your participation is voluntary and should be appreciated as such.

5. Pertinent technique: Refer to your ultimate decision maker. This allows you to avoid getting caught up in the emotions and, in doing so, compromise your chances for a win-win negotiation.

REVIEW

BEFORE HAND:

1. Know what you want and don't want
2. Research (Don't make off the cuff remarks.)
3. Timing

THE MATTER AT HAND:

1. Control your ego. The No. 1 enemy to a negotiation -- if you're emotionally distraught, chances are your ego is not in check.

2. Determine their needs. If you can determine someone's needs, you know what you want, and you have your ego in check, chances are you will achieve a win-win negotiation.

3. Be prepared to walk away. Make sure that people value your participation in a negotiation and under stand that it is not to be taken for granted.

Joseph A. Caruso

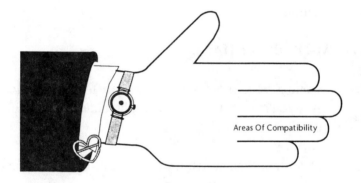

Areas Of Compatibility

Chapter 7

LOOK FOR AREAS OF COMPATIBILITY
(Ring Finger)

The fourth factor that you should consider in your efforts to achieve a win-win negotiation is represented by the ring finger. *Look for areas of compatibility.* As Lily Tomlin says, "We are all in this alone...together." We are all human beings. Even if you are negotiating with people whom you feel are your exact opposites -- in terms of personality, in terms of what's important in life or in terms of how they feel about people -- you should still be able to find some areas of compatibility. If you didn't feel you both had areas of common interest, you wouldn't be sitting down together to negotiate. Think about it. At the beginning of the negotiation, you determined what you wanted. If these people didn't have what you wanted, or at least the ability to provide you with it, you wouldn't be negotiating with them.

If you still don't believe that you have anything in common with your counterparts, consider this: If you're sincerely interested in achieving a win-win negotiation, you are definitely interested in seeing that your counterparts get what they want. In almost all of the cases, your counterparts will definitely be interested in making sure they get at least what they want. Therein lies your area of commonality or compatibility: YOU BOTH WANT *THEM* TO WIN.

Consequently, it's very important to remember the rule of thumb (get it?) and keep your ego in check. The most interesting element of any situation for all people is, "what's in it for me...what does this mean to me." If you can hone in on this, you will probably be able to find a number of areas of compatibility. (If this section sounds a lot like Chapter 5, "Determine Needs Of Others," you're right. The differences are sometimes subtle and both strategies comprise the heart of negotiation.) Listen actively and pay attention to detail. Also, encourage *them* to explore areas of compatibility. For example, invite them to put themselves in your position by asking, "Can you see the position I'm in? Can you see how this is? What would you do if you were me?"

If you feel you have no areas of compatibility, start making statements like, "When I say blank, it seems to demonstate that I don't care about this. I hear your concern about that." This way, you're not admitting that you don't care; you're saying that you share the concern.

In an instance like this, your area of compatibility does not lie in the actions, but in the perception of the actions. Your perceived sincerity will make your comments much more believable in your counterparts' eyes. Then continue..."You and I both want this resolved. That's why we're both here. What can we do to reach an agreement and solve this problem?" Continue to use questions instead of statements. Continue to separate people from the problem. Don't be diverted from the negotiation by the urge to teach your counterparts a lesson. Focus on their interests, not their positions.

REVIEW

Look For Areas Of Compatibility

1. Look for areas of compatibility.

2. Remember that both you and your counterparts want them to win. This is one definite area of compatibility.

3. If your counterparts feel you are on the opposite side of the fence, in terms of your actions, refer to your intentions and possible interpretations of the actions.

4. Ask questions and encourage suggestions.

Five Ways to Get the Upper Hand Every Time

Joseph A. Caruso

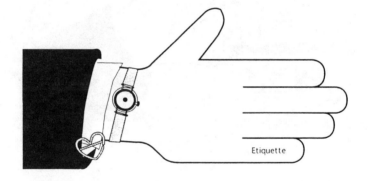

Etiquette

73

Chapter 8

USE ETIQUETTE
(Little Finger)

The fifth and final element essential to a win-win negotiation is the *use of etiquette*. This is represented by the little finger.

It is very important, throughout the negotiation, that you respect your counterparts' pride, ego, sentiment, values and positions. The minute they feel you don't respect them, you can expect contrary behavior, ideas, postures and positions from them.

I've given you several techniques to help you communicate the fact that you respect them and genuinely care about them on a realistic level. Make sure they understand that your purpose in negotiating with them is not to be unreasonable, manipulative, or to force them to compromise their integrity. You're also not there to get anything from them that is greater than what you're going to provide for them. Emerson said,

Joseph A. Caruso

"The music that can reach and cure all ills is cordial speech."

There are several techniques you can use to ensure you are using the proper amount of etiquette in your negotiations. One of the most important and effective techniques dictates that you never give away anything without putting a value on it.

EXAMPLE: Can you remember negotiating for something and getting exactly what you wanted upon your first request? How did you feel? I'll bet that, rather than feeling like you won, you felt like you should have asked for more.

You owe it to your counterparts not to leave them with this feeling. Even if you did get everything you wanted, make sure they know you respect them. If you do, there's a much greater likelihood that they will be true to the parameters of the agreement. This can be achieved in two ways: Never accept their first offer, and, again, never give anything away without putting a value on it.

Montaigne said, "People are not so much hurt by what happens, as by their opinions of what happens." Be sure that when you "give" something to your counterparts, they appreciate the value of the concession and feel obligated to give something in return. Roger Dawson, author of *Secrets of*

Five Ways to Get the Upper Hand Every Time

Power Negotiation, calls this the "Call Girl Principle." According to this principle, the value of the service depreciates greatly with time, once the service has been performed.

The solution to this, obviously, is to state the value immediately. If they're negotiating for a specific point, no matter how much they down-play the importance of the point, the fact is they want it. If you give it away first, *then* try to put a value on it, your counterparts will probably tell you that they really didn't want it that bad. In fact, they may go even further and say that, if they'd known you were going to ask that much, they probably wouldn't have requested it. The simple solution is to *agree to the value* of each concession before you make it. Otherwise, you will lose.

Here's a funny anecdote regarding the value of something: Recently, a group of sports writers were perplexed at what they perceived to be the shrinking strike-zone in baseball. The writers decided to contact the top three home plate umpires and ask them one question: "What is a strike?" Their answers were enlightening. The first umpire replied, "I calls 'em as I sees 'em." The second umpire replied, "I calls 'em as they are." The third umpire replied, "They ain't nothin' 'til I calls 'em."

I live by the third philosophy. It is impossible for anyone to guess the personal value you place on the specific concessions you make during a negotiation. With each concession, make sure your counterparts fully realize its value to you. You'll find this technique to be incredibly useful in virtually all of the elements of your negotiation.

Another aspect in negotiation finesse is letting your counterparts know what good negotiators they were throughout the negotiation. Take every opportunity to let them know that you respect them as human beings (even though you may not respect their position, approach or style). Once the negotiation is completed, let them know how glad you are that you were able to come to an agreement, but also how they didn't make things easy for you. Tell them they drove a hard bargain, but you respect them for it. This will help make them feel good about the agreement they made with you. Consequently, they'll be more likely to want to negotiate with you in the future -- *and* they'll be more likely to keep their side of the negotiated settlement.

<u>REVIEW</u>

Use Etiquette:

1. Let your counterparts know how much you respect them.

2. Never give away anything without first putting a value on it.

3. State the value immediately.

4. Agree to the value of each concession "before hand."

5. Let your counterparts know what good negotiators they were at the close of the negotiation.

Joseph A. Caruso

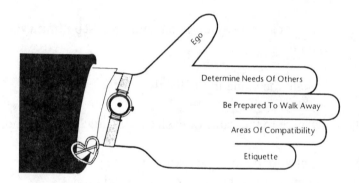

Section III

CHANGING FOR GOOD
(Holding Your Hand)

Joseph A. Caruso

Chapter 9

POWER OF HABIT

"Habit is habit, and not to be flung out of the window by any man, but coaxed down the stairs a step at a time." -- Mark Twain.

You will find it almost impossible to successfully apply the information you have learned in this book if you aren't aware of the power of habit in your life. It's been said that, "If you always do what you've always done, you'll get what you've always gotten." If you're sincerely looking to improve your "happiness factor" by becoming more success-ful with your interpersonal communication, you will need to address those habits that you want to change.

There are six basic steps to developing a habit.

1. *You must desire change.* Change is a necessary part of growth. The German philosopher Hegel said, "Struggle is the law of growth, character is built in the storm and stress of the world; and a person reaches his full height only through com-

pulsions, responsibilities, and suffering." You must really *believe* that, if you do change your habit, you will be richly rewarded for your efforts. The change that will happen in your life by replacing your old habits with positive new ones should be promising and exciting enough to make the necessary efforts worthwhile.

2. *You must develop a strong dislike for your current habit.* Analyze the particular behavioral traits or sequence of events that are responsible for perpetuating your existing conditions. Learn to look at these perpetual behavioral traits as the enemy. If they're not defeated, you can't succeed in your desire to grow. For example, if your ego starts to get in the way in a negotiation, and you feel yourself getting angry, don't use trite, meaningless excuses like, "I have a right to be angry," or, "Well, he/she just pushed my button." Instead, redirect your energy toward efforts to stop slipping into your old ways. Recognize these old habits as your enemy. Develop a strong will to not let them creep into your behavior. *You* are the boss. You're in charge of your own actions.

3. *You must be consistent in your approach.* You've given your whole life to be who you are right now. Think about it. If you want to effect a major change in a particular behavior pattern, it will take a sincere and concentrated effort. Just as a person cannot expect to become a nonsmoker by giving up an occa-

Five Ways to Get the Upper Hand Every Time

sional cigarette, you can't expect tremendous results by *occasionally* improving one or two communication skills. Don't get frustrated by the immensity of the task. Simply keep in mind, as Blythe said, "The most important thing in the world is always what a man is doing at this moment."

4. Along with being consistent in your approach, it is just as important that *your approach be consistent with your personality*. A situation one of my brothers once found himself in can be used to illustrate this point. He felt that he was putting on a little extra weight and wasn't as physically fit as he wanted to be, so he decided that every day he would start working out in the basement with weights. He was fairly successful with this for about a week and a half. He told everyone how great he felt and how everyone should be exercising regularly. Soon, however, days would pass without him working out. He found many reasons to justify his inability to keep his commitment. He was still just as unhappy with his physical condition, and his desire to change was just as strong. The problem was his means for changing were not consistent with his personality. He prefers to do things with people, rather than alone. Eventually he came to the conclusion that he might have better luck if, during the winter months, rather than working out alone, he'd play racquetball once or twice a week with his friends. The results were extremely positive. He played racquetball at least

once a week consistently throughout the winter season. He was able to keep his commitment *and* reach his goal.

5. *You must have patience.* If you're the type of person who needs to see immediate results in order to stick with the project, I recommend you set "mini-goals" or "mile markers." Rather than dreaming of the day when you will have completely broken the old habits, focus your efforts on one day, one hour or one opportunity at a time. Take every opportunity to replace your old behavioral techniques with these new communication techniques. See each occasion that you do so successfully as a victory, but realize that each victory is just one battle in a long war. Go ahead and celebrate each victory, even share it with your friends if you like. Congratulate yourself for having the tenacity, fortitude and presence of mind to not only recognize your old behavioral patterns creeping in, but to successfully replace them with these new techniques.

CAUTION: Don't use occasional victories as an excuse to justify letting the next opportunity slip by. This would be like the man who, in his efforts to lose weight, jogged one mile on his first day and rewarded himself with an entire bag of cookies.

6. *Analyze past obstacles.* Determine the things in the past that kept you from achieving your desired goals and objectives.

Five Ways to Get the Upper Hand Every Time

Create ways to effectively deal with these obstacles if they were to reoccur. If you've found times in the past when you were unsuccessful at keeping the commitments necessary to experience long-term changes in your life, it's not very likely the problem occurred at the beginning of your efforts. These aren't the moments you need to analyze in order to be more successful this time. Rather, isolate and analyze the obstacles and hurdles that you felt, as well as the excuses you used, when you *stopped* trying to inject your life with these "new" behaviors. Keep the following passage in mind as you investigate and isolate those moments.

> *In all investigations, the answers you get depend on the questions you ask: the questions you ask depend on the assumptions you make, and the assumptions you make depend on how much you think you know. Even more on how much you take for granted and most of all, in serious investigations, on how willing you are to accept what William James called "the pain of a new idea." --Renee Haynes*

Once you've identified your trouble spots, think of what you will do this time to render those excuses helpless, thus enabling you to continue with your commitment. Keep in mind that change is not always easy. However, it's the most

difficult times in your life that offer your greatest opportunity for growth.

Chapter 10

DECISION VS. COMMITMENT

"Change and growth take place only when a person has risked himself and dared to become involved with experimenting with his own mind." --Herbert Otto

There is a difference between a decision and a commitment. Commitment is based in passion. Emerson said, "Nothing great in the world was ever accomplished without passion."

Don't confuse habits that were "learned" with instinct. Since I don't want to force anyone to become an amateur psychologist just to make this distinction, perhaps this quote from Spinoza will be enough to make my point: "Instincts are magnificent as a driving force, but dangerous as guides; for by what we may call individualism of the instincts, each of them seeks its own fulfillment, regardless of the good of the whole personality. To be ourselves, we must complete ourselves."

Joseph A. Caruso

The people who read this book and want to apply the ideas in their own lives could be divided into two categories:

1. Those who were able to improve their negotiation skills.
2. Those who were not.

There will be one -- and only one -- definitive difference between these two groups of people. Specifically, the people in the second group merely made a *decision* to apply the information they read in this book, while the people in the first group made a *commitment* to apply the information.

Millions of dollars have been spent on books that promise to teach people how to lose weight. And throughout modern history, millions of pounds have been lost by people around the world, using hundreds of different techniques. The results of an informal poll once taken among people who were able to keep the weight off is quite telling. The overwhelming majority of the people said the No. 1 reason they were able to lose weight and keep it off had more to do with their personal commitment than the specific technique they used.

The road will be difficult at first. Decisions are fine for the short term. However, it is the commitment that will take you the distance. You will find that as time goes on your tenacity will be rewarded because it will become increasingly easier to incorporate your new habit into your daily life.

Noted author Brian Tracy uses an excellent example in

Five Ways to Get the Upper Hand Every Time

his tape series, *The Psychology of Selling*:

EXAMPLE: There's only one time in the entire flight of commercial airplanes where the pilot must push the throttle all the way to its limits; where the entire thrust of the engines is necessary...that is upon take-off. There isn't another moment throughout the flight where the engines get forced to their maximum capacity. It's simply not necessary.

It's the same with changing habits. If you make a commitment rather than a decision to change, it will be much more difficult, at first, to incorporate these positive new changes in your everyday life than it will be later on, once they have crept into your personality. (The laws of inertia must, at least, be somewhat applicable to behavior.)

I encourage you to make a 21-day effort to incorporate the basic philosophies (represented by the visual symbols in the illustrations) at every opportunity in your interpersonal relationships. I'm confident that two things will happen:
1. The reward for your efforts will be great enough that you'll want to continue and strengthen your efforts.
2. You'll find it increasingly easier to stop old and negative behaviors and replace them with your new, positive approaches.

Joseph A. Caruso

Many people, right now, are experiencing happier lives because they've been able to successfully implement the approaches and ideas in this book. In the words of Herbert Otto, I invite you to, "experiment with your own mind." You stand to lose nothing but your efforts. Renew your promise every morning to apply these techniques. Cut out the last page of this book and tape it to your mirror. Review it every morning and remind yourself to take every opportunity to apply these techniques throughout the day. If this approach is too general for you, I encourage you to focus in on either the ego (thumb), or on determining the needs of others (index finger). These two areas will provide you with the most immediate and noticeable results. They are the cornerstones and the most essential elements to win-win negotiation.

At life's end, we are left with either excuses or results. Think about this statement each time you think you have an *excuse* to cheat yourself out of the opportunity to change negative and old behavioral patterns.

I wish you well in your efforts and I remind you of the words of Moltiere, "It is not only what we do, but what we do not do for which we are accountable."

Section IV

WORDS OF WISDOM
(A Helping Hand)

Joseph A. Caruso

Chapter 11

WORDS OF WISDOM

Your success in applying the techniques for win-win negotiation in your daily life will be based largely upon your philosophies and approaches to negotiation, your attitude about yourself and your respect for others. This section is a collection of what I've found to be pertinent, motivating, inspirational or provocative thoughts stated in very concise language.

Quotations sometimes serve as the justification of our beliefs or the inspiration of our goals. I encourage you to pick your favorite quotes, or the ones you think will have the greatest effect on helping you achieve your goals, and write them on a piece of paper. Then, either memorize them or post them in a place where you spend a great deal of time (the kitchen, your workplace, etc.) so they may serve as a reminder for your personal objectives.

Enjoy!

Joseph A. Caruso

There is only one way to happiness, and that is cease worrying about things which are beyond the power of our will.
--Epictetus

Life does not consist mainly -- or even largely -- of facts and happenings. It consists mainly of the storm of thoughts that is forever blowing through one's head.
--Mark Twain

The heights by great men reached and kept were not attained by sudden flight, but they, while their companions slept, were tolling upward in the night.
--Henry Wodsworth Longfellow

Experience shows that success is due less to ability than to zeal. The winner is he who gives himself to his work, body and soul.
--Charles Buxton

Five Ways to Get the Upper Hand Every Time

As you think, you travel; and as you love you attract. You are today where your thoughts have brought you; you will be tomorrow where your thoughts take you. You cannot escape the result of your thoughts, but you can endure and learn...
You will realize the vision (not the idle wish) of your heart, be it base or beautiful...
For you will always gravitate towards that which you, secretly, most love. Whatever your present environment may be, you will fall, remain, or rise with your thoughts, your vision, your ideal. You will become as small as your controlling desire: as great as your dominant aspiration.
--James Allen

Success
To laugh often and much; to win the respect of intelligent people and affection of children; to earn the appreciation of honest critics and endure the betrayal of false friends; to appreciate beauty, to find the best in others; to leave the world a bit better, whether by a healthy child, a garden patch or a redeemed social condition; to know even one life has breathed easier because you have lived. This is to have succeeded.
--Ralph Waldo Emerson

Joseph A. Caruso

<u>The Promise</u>

I promise myself to be strong, that nothing can disturb my peace of mind. To talk health, happiness and prosperity to every person I meet. To make my friends feel that there is something good in them. To look on the sunny side of everything and make my optimism come true. To think the best, work only for the best and accept only the best. To forget the mistakes of the past and press on to the greater achievements of the future. To give so much time to the improvement of myself that I have no time to criticize others. To be too large for worry, too noble for anger, too strong for fear and too happy to permit the presence of trouble. To think well of myself and proclaim this fact to the world, not in loud words but in great deeds. To live in the faith that the world is on my side as long as I am true to the best in me.

--Spinoza

To hate is to acknowledge our inferiority and our fear. We do not hate a foe who we are confident we can overcome.

--Spinoza

Five Ways to Get the Upper Hand Every Time

...for a conscious being, to exist is to change, to change is to mature, to mature is to go on creating one's self endlessly.
--Henri Bergson, 1859-1941
  French Philosopher, Nobel Prize

There are in fact four very significant stumbling blocks in the way of grasping the truth, which hinder every man however learned, and scarcely allow anyone to win a clear title to wisdom, namely, the example of weak and unworthy authority, long standing custom, the feeling of the ignorant crowd, and the hiding of our own ignorance while making a display of our apparent knowledge.
--Roger Bacon, 1220-1292

Do what you can, with what you have, where you are.
--Theodore Roosevelt

Joseph A. Caruso

The best soldier does not attack. The superior fighter succeeds without violence. The greatest conqueror wins without a struggle. The most successful manager leads without dictating. This is called intelligent non-aggressiveness. This is called mastery of men.
--Lao Tzu

One who is too insistent on his views, finds few to agree with him.
--Lao Tzu

Every man alone is sincere. At the entrance of a second person, hypocrisy begins.
--Ralph Waldo Emerson

We are afraid of truth, afraid of fortune, afraid of death and afraid of each other...we are parlor soldiers. We shun the rugged battle of fate, where strength is born.
--Ralph Waldo Emerson

Five Ways to Get the Upper Hand Every Time

A wise person learns to treasure the trophy as much as they cherish the chase.
--Joe Caruso

If one advances confidently, in the direction of his own dreams and endeavors, to lead the life which he has imagined, he will meet with a success unexpected in common hours.
--Henry David Thoreau

In terms of balancing human values, I would give the enjoyment of life first priority and justify that on the grounds that if you don't know how to enjoy life, you're going to be a burden to other people.
--Nevitt Sanford

To venture is to cause anxiety. But not to venture is to lose oneself.
--Ralph Waldo Emerson

Joseph A. Caruso

What lies behind us and what lies before us are tiny matter compared to what lies within us.
--Ralph Waldo Emerson

We learn to speak by speaking; we learn to run by running; we learn to love by loving; there is no other way.
--St. Francis De Sales

If you can imagine it, you can achieve it. If you can dream it, you can become it.
--William Arthur Ward

It is not easy to find happiness in ourselves, and it's not possible to find it elsewhere.
--Agnes Repplier

Don't be afraid your life will end; be afraid that it will never begin.
--Grace Hansen

Five Ways to Get the Upper Hand Every Time

We are here to add what we can to life, not to get what we can from it.
--William Oslar

Adversity introduces a person to themselves.
--Joe Caruso

The size of a person can be measured by the size of the thing that makes them angry.
--James Allen

What you are speaks so loudly that I cannot hear what you say.
--Ralph Waldo Emerson

Worrying is the interest you pay on a debt you may never owe.
--Joe Caruso

Guilt is an effective parent, but an awful teacher.
--Joe Caruso

Joseph A. Caruso

It is the commonest of mistakes to consider that the limit of our power of perception is also the limit of all that there is to perceive.
--C.W. Leadbeater

Most of us spend a lot of time dreaming of the future, never realizing a little arrives each day.
--Joe Caruso

We don't remember days, we remember moments. Our efforts then should lie, not in 'having a good day,' but in 'creating a nice moment.'
--Joe Caruso

From the lowliest depths there is a path to the loftiest heights.
--Joe Caruso

Five Ways to Get the Upper Hand Every Time

It's not the amount or type of problems that you have, but the way you go about overcoming them that determines your character.
--Joe Caruso

Champion's Creed
I am not judged by the number of times I fail, but by the number of times I succeed. And the number of times I succeed, is in direct proportion with the number of times I fail and keep trying.

The greatest risk in life is to wait for and depend upon others for your security. The greatest security is to plan and act and take the risk that will make you independent.
--Denis Waitley

This above all: to thine own self be true, and it must follow, as the night the day, thou canst not then be false to any man.
--Shakespeare

Joseph A. Caruso

The feeling of being hurried is not usually the result of living a full life and having no time. It is, rather of a vague fear that we are wasting our life.
--Eric Hoffer

Five Ways to Get the Upper Hand Every Time

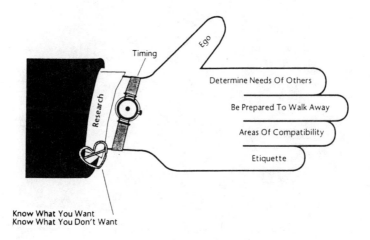

About the Author

Joe Caruso is a dynamic and inspirational speaker who has helped thousands achieve individual excellence and higher levels of success and productivity. He is considered a guru on the subject of change and transition.

As an author, Joe has experience with a wide range of topics. He has written three books and his popular newspaper column, *Success Strategies*, is read by hundreds of thousands.

As a speaker, Joe's techniques for motivation and productivity, as well as his courses on transition, have revolutionized the industry and have been embraced by some of the most successful corporations and associations in the world.

As an adviser, Joe is co-founder of CarusoKlemans International Development Institute, a respected leader in the areas of training and development. He considers himself an *ex-expert*. **"Rather than being an expert,"** says Joe, **"I <u>choose</u> to be effective."**

About the
CarusoKlemans
International
Development Institute

CarusoKlemans International Development Institute, founded by Joseph Caruso and Barbara Klemans, is respected as a leader in the areas of training and development.

CarusoKlemans International Development Institute is <u>consistently effective</u> in helping corporations and associations achieve positive and long-lasting results in the areas of communication, management training, change and transition, negotiations and productivity.

Our mission is: *to develop our skills and knowledge to the best of our ability to help people and corporations experience the greatest possible success.*

for more information contact:
CarusoKlemans, Ltd.
3171 Palmetto Court
Trenton, Michigan 48183
(313) 692-0544

Courses Available include:

12 Steps to Effective Meetings

5 Ways to Get the Upper Hand Every Time

The Inner Game of Management

Creating Enjoyment in the Workplace

Creating a Ninja Sales Force

Turning a Group into a Team

Get What You Want & Enjoy the Process

Yes, You Can Get There From Here

Other Books Available:

12 Steps to Effective Meetings

Success Strategies

Clients include:

American Heart Association
ASC, Inc.
Cellular One
Charter National Bank
Dearborn Federal Credit Union
First of America Bank
Ford Motor Company
Holiday Inn
Hotel Sales & Marketing Association
Mazda Motors of America
Meeting Professionals International
Northwest Airlines, Inc.
Ramada Corporation
Residence Inn
Society of Association Executives
Society of Manufacturing Engineers